DECK
THE
HALLS

Calendar for 1908

The Welcome

May friendly faces
be ever near
And loving voices
your way to cheer.

"I will honor Christmas
and try to keep it in
my heart all the year."

CHARLES DICKENS

DECK THE HALLS

BY ROBERT·M·MERCK

ABBEVILLE PRESS · PUBLISHERS

NEW YORK · LONDON · PARIS

DEDICATION

To my mother and father, Dolores and Mel,
and my brother Tim, who made my childhood
Christmases so special, and who continue to personify
the spirit of Christmas every day
of the year.

Editor: Walton Rawls
Designer: Jos. Trautwein
Copy Chief: Robin James
Production Supervisor: Hope Koturo

Library of Congress Cataloging-in-Publication Data
Merck, Robert M.
Deck the halls / by Robert M. Merck
p.   cm.
ISBN 1-55859-267-9
I. Christmas decorations.   I. Title.
NK4696.4.M47   1992
745.594'12—dc 20   92-23731
CIP

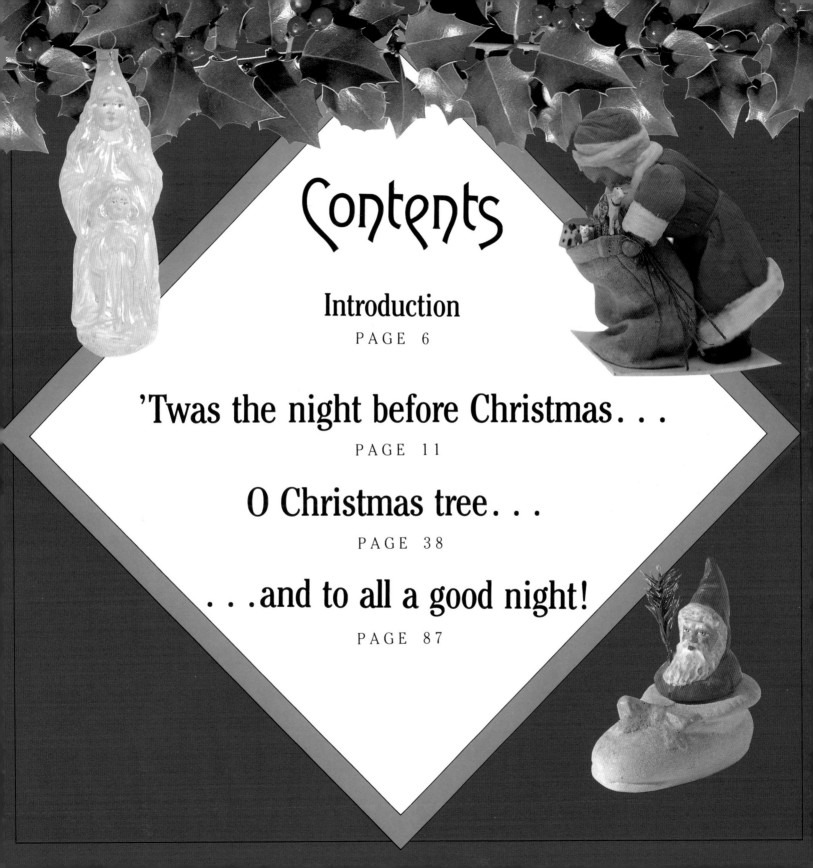

Contents

h . . . Christmas! Few words conjure up such rich images of childhood fantasy and fond memories. Fragrant green boughs, mulled cider, twinkling lights, swirling snowflakes, Santa Claus, unseen surprises wrapped in bright packages, favorite carols sung by a roaring fire, and countless other traditions warm the heart at this favorite time of year.

The magic of Christmas links generations. Your grandmother's house at Christmas might be one of your fondest childhood memories. Perhaps you still own and cherish a small clip-on glass-bird ornament from her tree. Or you traditionally prepare the same time-honored holiday recipes you remember as a child. Most of us still take great delight in sharing a child's exhilaration in anticipating the arrival of Santa Claus, since we, too, are transfixed by the excitement of his presence. Christmas has been called the "day of days," and its magic, combined with our memories, makes December 25th a joyous occasion that inspires us all through the year.

Although Christmas was widely celebrated throughout America for much of the nineteenth century, it was not until 1890 that all states recognized December 25th as a legal holiday. By then, the old German custom of decorating a tree as part of the celebration of Christ's birth had spread worldwide.

Trees and boughs in the early nineteenth century were bedecked with cookies, apples, nuts, and sparkling cones made of paper and colored foil in which one could place small confections. Special almond- or spice-flavored cookie dough was often pressed into a carved wooden mold for baking, the result being a cookie that looked like a flower, bird, or animal. By the mid nineteenth century, popcorn was being strung on thread to serve as snowlike garlands on the tree. Strings of dried apple slices as well as cranberries added to the merriment. The use of these goodies as decorations made taking down the tree, traditionally on Twelfth Night, a small, tasty feast.

During the late 1800s, paper ornaments became the rage. Fancy scraps of colored paper and embossed gold and silver trims were meticulously assembled by Victorian ladies and their children into hearts, banners, snowflakes, and the like. With the development of chromolithography in England, and its instant popularity in Germany, spectacularly detailed and colorful embossed-paper images or "scraps" flooded the American market. By attaching gold metallic bands of Christmas tinsel roping to favorite lithographed images, lovely tree trimmings were born.

Around this time, decorations for the tree that could be purchased commercially began to appear. Not surprisingly, it was Germany that supplied the majority of the sparkling ornaments and whimsies that decorated the American home

during the holidays. These decorations, fashioned of tin, wax, glass, cotton, paper, or papier-mâché, were made by cottage-industry workers in small villages located primarily in the Thuringian mountains of Germany.

At the same time that toys and ornaments were being produced in quantity for the American market, German toymakers began creating Santa Claus figures for decorating the mantel or to stand guard next to a tabletop Christmas tree. These images, made of papier-mâché or a composition of pressed paper pulp and glue, were slender old men dressed in robes covered with fine mica flakes or "snow." Early figures often had a stern expression, and instead of carrying a Christmas tree or wrapped packages they held switches with which to punish bad boys and girls. Santa Claus and his counterparts (Kris Kringle, Belsnickel, Father Christmas, and St. Nicholas) always have been simultaneously loved and somewhat feared by children. Just as today, parents in Victorian times used Santa Claus as a disciplinary force throughout the year to remind children to be good and mind their manners.

For much of the nineteenth century, Christmas trees were illuminated by snow-white candles placed on the ends of the branches. On Christmas morning, the

adults gathered in the parlor, and as the doors were slid open the sight was breathtaking for the children as they first beheld the tree laden with flickering candles.

It took only three years after Thomas Edison invented the electric light bulb before his new technology appeared on a Christmas tree. In 1882, the first electrically lit Christmas tree was turned on in New York City, and it featured small glass light-globes in red, white, and blue. Word of the beauty of electric lights for the tree spread rapidly, and as electric power became more widely available the demand among wealthy homeowners for festoons of colored lights at Christmas grew accordingly.

What is it about Christmas that we cherish? Perhaps it is the uncomplicated innocence of childhood and the wonders the holiday bestows on us all. From earliest memory many of us have carried a vision of Christmas past. The warm recollections of bygone celebrations encourage us to strive to make each Christmas "the best ever." Antique Christmas decorations capture the beauty and happiness of yesteryear. Each of us, by saving our family's Christmas treasures from year to year, helps preserve the traditions and magic of this very special season.

'Twas the night before Christmas . . .

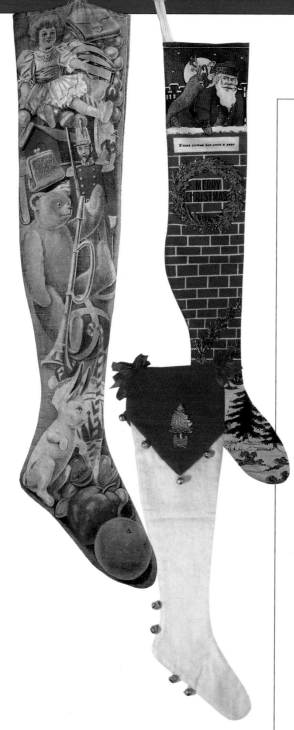

Printed-fabric Christmas stockings were sold in sheets ready to be cut out and assembled at home. Victorian ladies also made stockings from materials they had on hand.

What would Christmas be without Santa Claus? It is difficult to imagine. This jolly old elf embodies the kindness and generosity that permeate celebrations of the holiday season. Our affection for him endures even beyond childhood fantasies, and his anticipated arrival each year is an integral part of the mystery and magic of Christmas.

For centuries, holiday celebrants have favored various versions of Santa Claus, each a festive gift-bearer but sometimes one who punished wrongdoers. The majority of Santa Claus images are based on St. Nicholas, the legendary bishop renowned as the patron saint of children. Said to have been a benefactor through gifts and glad tidings all year, St. Nicholas still visits small children with gifts and sweets in Germany on December 6, his feast day.

In parts of Germany, Santa Claus was known as Pelz Nichol, or "Santa in Fur." A variant of this name was common in nineteenth-century German settlements in America, predominantly in Pennsylvania. There, "Belsnickel" would visit on Christmas Eve, bearing gifts or leaving switches or a lump of coal for bad boys and girls.

Out of the German toy industry in the late 1800s emerged papier-mâché figures of Santa Claus and Belsnickel for the American market. Santa Claus figures were crafted in most mediums, but usually they had a papier-mâché or composition

Ready to set out on his Christmas Eve journey, Santa Claus and his sleigh (above) are pulled by his trusted reindeer. Removing the reindeer's head reveals a secret compartment for candy and treats.

The sleigh and reindeer below, measuring four feet in length, were likely a store display in the early part of the twentieth century.

body, head, hands, and boots, and were dressed in a hooded robe trimmed in lambswool or felt. Some carried a tiny woven-wicker basket at the waist or on the back, and most had a candy container of cylindrical cardboard concealed under a long robe.

Belsnickel figures were made of chalk or papier-mâché with painted robes in white, red, blue, green, and other colors. Often sprinkled with fine mica-dust "snow," they carried a tiny green tree sprig or small switches in the crook of an arm. Belsnickels were marketed in America at the turn of the century as candy containers or table and mantel decorations, selling for a few cents each.

In 1822, Clement Moore had written "A Visit From St. Nicholas." Subsequently, Thomas Nast, the famed political cartoonist, depicted Santa Claus from the 1860s on as an elfin figure navigating a sleigh pulled by eight tiny reindeer. It is this image that we still hold dear more than one hundred years later as we look forward to the "day of days."

Even though they were fragile, these Santa toys were mounted on a sturdy platform with wheels, so they could be pulled through the house by the children.

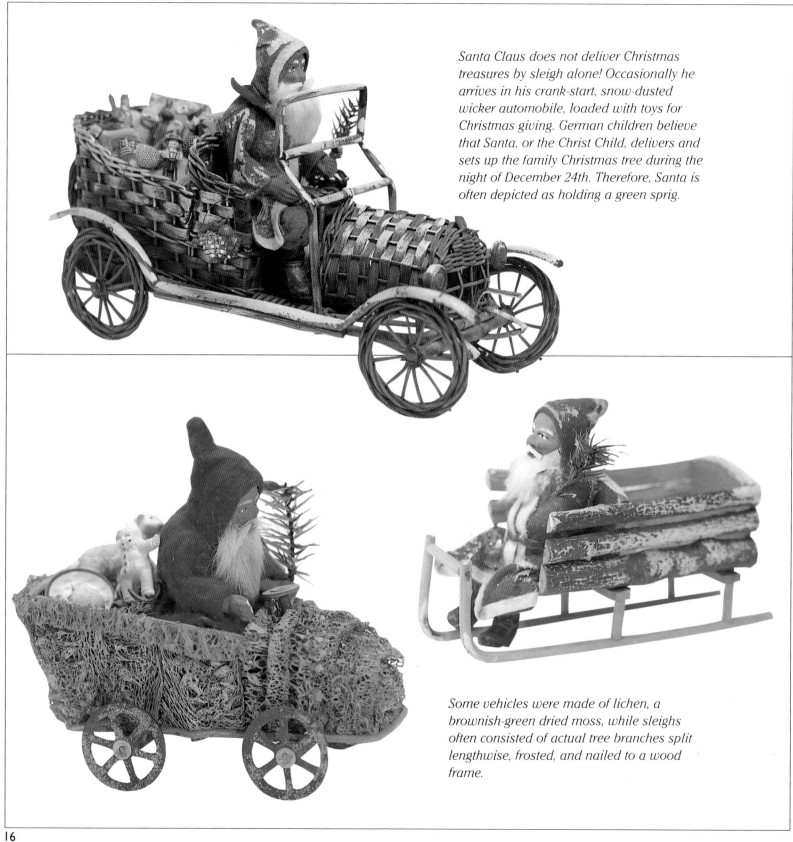

Santa Claus does not deliver Christmas treasures by sleigh alone! Occasionally he arrives in his crank-start, snow-dusted wicker automobile, loaded with toys for Christmas giving. German children believe that Santa, or the Christ Child, delivers and sets up the family Christmas tree during the night of December 24th. Therefore, Santa is often depicted as holding a green sprig.

Some vehicles were made of lichen, a brownish-green dried moss, while sleighs often consisted of actual tree branches split lengthwise, frosted, and nailed to a wood frame.

Turn-of-the-century Christmas decorations, like toys of the era, were often crafted in the cottages of German workers. They would assemble the parts and piece goods in their homes for local merchants who would then export the finished products to the United States. The clothing and general appearance of Santa figures varied according to local customs, beliefs, and available materials. One Santa might look like a carpenter or more like a woodsman or be presented with stern visage in white fur riding a donkey. The tradition of St. Nicholas riding through town on a donkey is still continued in Germany today. On St. Nicholas Day, December 6th, many villagers honor the arrival of this patron saint, who parades through the town square showering small children with fancily wrapped foil-covered chocolates.

The stern fellow in the center at left holds a crying child in his bag, for it was believed that Santa Claus would carry off boys and girls who did not behave during the year. The Santa in the pink robe is a squeak toy; when his shoulders are pressed down, a spring bellows under his robe emits a peeping sound.

Santa Claus figures in robes other than red are scarce, and reflect the varying traditions observed in different parts of Germany in the late 1800s. Most Santas served as candy boxes, with a cardboard cylinder hidden beneath their robes that slides apart to reveal the sweets.

Below: *Just as today, early images of Santa frequently frighten young children, who fear reprimands for bad deeds.*

19

Below: *Copyrighted in 1882, this folding advertising card appears to be a flat, latched box that reads, when closed, "A Christmas Box . . . Where's Santa Claus?" Santa appears when the card is opened, also revealing the name of the store that gave the card to its customers as a promotional tool.*

HERE HE IS!

COMPLIMENTS OF

Forbes & Wallace,

SPRINGFIELD,

MASS.

Santa Claus plays with two dressed-up dancing dogs in this unusual lithographed paper "die-cut."

Two Santas travel down the road in their automobile, delivering Christmas cheer.

The invention of color lithography permitted artists to create lavishly colored images on paper, and die-cut decorations and advertisements soon became commonplace. Some, like the image at left, included a space in which a merchant could insert the name of his store.

Some lithographed paper images were created for framing, or more commonly were intended for children to glue into their scrapbooks on a cold winter's evening. The majority of quality lithographed paper was produced in Germany at the turn of the century, but American and British craftsmen also showed much talent in this craft.

Printed by the Henry S. Dole Company of Chicago in 1883, this happy fellow straddles a yule log. The string threaded through his hands makes him a charming decoration for hanging on the tree.

Imagine the excitement felt by the lucky turn-of-the-century child who found this twenty-eight-inch Santa pull-toy on Christmas morning! Made of papier-mâché with jointed arms and neck, he is mounted on a platform with wheels.

Equipped with a lighted tree and lantern, Santa is well-prepared for his snowy journey. Ladened with tiny packages, the fellow below sports a wooden carrier on his back, commonly used in Germany years ago to help a person carry large loads comfortably.

The image of Santa varied widely in the late 1800s. Hailing from the Lancaster, Pennsylvania, area in the 1870s, the fellow at left is a classic "Belsnickel," with glass eyes and wooden teeth. At right is a Russian-looking Santa bundled up in a black lambswool-trimmed robe.

Wearing an unusual lambswool hat, the Father Christmas below holds wooden switches with which to punish naughty children and carries a basket full of tiny wooden toys on his back for good boys and girls.

Patented in 1876, the oil lamp above was made in America. The snowball base held oil, and the wick emerged inside Santa's robe. When lit, the lamp imbued the room with a soft glow.

Upper left: *German-made Father Christmas figures, c. 1910. Each has a cardboard cylinder hidden under his robe that holds candy.*

Left: *Papier-mâché and plaster lanterns. When a candle was lit inside, the paper facial inserts would be illuminated. Such lanterns were hung on the tree or carried on a stick by a child when caroling during the holidays.*

This colorful Christmas book (above and below right) is die-cut in the shape of Santa's head. When opened, each page of the book is slightly wider than the previous one. This adds an additional facial feature to the profile, so when the book is closed the head and face are complete. It was published in Germany by Saalfield Publishing Company in the early 1900s.

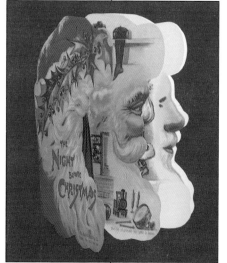

Children's Christmas books from around 1900 (above and right) were lavishly illustrated. "The Night before Christmas" was one of the most popular titles.

Most early Santa Claus books sold for only a few cents, despite their full-color illustrations. The most prolific publisher was McLoughlin Brothers of New York.

In Victorian times, even scrapbooks were manufactured with Santa Claus on the cover. The two dark-covered books at right were made in 1876 and contained blank pages to which a child could glue colorful die-cut or scrap paper images.

The tradition of sending greeting cards to family and friends at Christmas has existed for more than one hundred years. Some of the postcards shown at left could be held to the light to reveal tiny cut-out images cleverly "hidden" in the picture. Merchants in the late 1800s gave away lavishly colored and embossed die-cuts or "trade cards" depicting Santa for gluing into the family scrap album.

Among the most elaborate Christmas greetings of the Victorian era are "fold-out" cards. When a flat fold-out card is opened, a three-dimensional picture pops up.

Left: *Sporting an unusual hat and standing on a snowball, this Belsnickel wears boots that separate from his robe to reveal a small box for candy.*

Chalkware Santas were made primarily in the German settlements of Pennsylvania. Often depicted as stern fellows carrying switches, these early figures likely frightened young and old alike. The unusually friendly Santa at the far left below has a small child on his shoulder.

Knecht Ruppert was believed to assist the Christ Child in compiling a list of deserving children to whom He would deliver gifts at Christmas.

Right: *This Santa's head nods up and down when touched. It is suspended on a wire and counterweighted with a lead pendulum below. The figure's boots pull out from his robe to reveal a cardboard tube designed to hold sweets.*

Bundled up in brown robes covered with "snow," these nineteenth-century Santas carry goose-feather Christmas trees decorated with tiny wax candles.

Ranging in size from 15 to 22 inches, this group of Belsnickels makes an imposing "family" portrait. Figures with rabbit-fur beards, switches, or a crown are uncommon.

Unusual due to their size, color, or form, each of these Belsnickels measures under six inches in height. Rare forms include those with wreaths in their hair, wearing a flat hat, or bundled up against cold winter weather with scarves over their mouths. Belsnickels in brown or black robes are particularly scarce.

Elaborate fold-out Christmas decorations were given to valued customers by shop owners advertising their wares at the turn of the century. Some were not only decorative but included a calendar for use throughout the year.

The 1904 calendar (lower left) combined the image of Santa Claus with angels and a reference to the Christ Child. The other two calendars were promotional pieces for the Theo. Gier Wine Co. of Oakland, California.

Fold-out paper nativity scenes were made in Germany for many years. They were sold as greeting cards for the holiday season or as mantel or table decorations. Although quite attractive when flat, they become almost lifelike when opened and the scene becomes three-dimensional.

Popular tiny surprises for Santa to leave in the stockings of good boys and girls included doll-size clothespins, pocket knives, whistles, jumping jacks, toy watches, and small hand puzzles.

Whether by land, sea, or air, Santa always manages to visit each home with his bag full of gifts.

Bisque "snowbabies," as they are commonly called, were made in Germany for many years. They were sold as table and under-the-tree village decorations, and were also used to decorate the tops of holiday cakes. Each standing only a few inches high, they are miniature depictions of the jolly old elf carrying out his mission.

O Christmas tree. . . .

Full of expectation and wonder, children are greeted Christmas morning by a tree lit with twinkling lights and bedecked with brightly colored ornaments, toys, and garlands. This magic moment is joyfully remembered throughout our lives. As one grows older, the moment can be recreated each year, oftentimes using the same decorations lovingly saved from Christmases past.

Not all trees were as elaborately decorated as this ten-foot tree belonging to the author. Its boughs are ladened with hundreds of antique decorations dating from as early as the 1880s. American flags were a traditional component of family celebrations in Victorian times, typifying a surge in patriotism. Even at Christmas a tree was not "complete" without a nod to national pride.

Sparkling like small jewels on the tree, figural glass ornaments were among the earliest and most popular decorations made in Germany. In the 1890s, F. W. Woolworth, known for his popular "five and ten cent" stores, discovered these fanciful baubles while on a toy and doll buying trip to Sonneberg, Germany. Wildly popular, these inexpensive but beautifully crafted ornaments are said to have contributed greatly to Mr. Woolworth's success.

In the tiny town of Lauscha, Germany, lies the birthplace of glass Christmas tree ornaments. Long known for producing fine-quality glassware, Lauschan artisans developed the first mouth-blown figural glass Christmas ornament in the last half of the nineteenth century.

Entire families were involved in the production of glass Christmas ornaments; even the children had specific duties. Laboring up to sixteen hours a day, six days a week, some families relied on producing ornaments as their sole source of income.

The creation of an ornament began with the heating of a clear glass tube over a flame to exactly the right temperature before it was inserted into a claylike figural mold. The father of the house would then quickly blow into the exposed end of the tube, causing the glass inside to expand and take on the form of the mold. When cooled, a silver nitrate solution was swirled inside the hollow glass form to give the figure a bright silver glow. Members of the family would then painstakingly apply the delicate paints, metal caps, and finishing touches to the figures.

Occasionally, contests were held in the village, with prizes awarded to the family producing the most original or attractive decorations. The designs created for American Christmas trees often reflected popular themes and characters of the time. Patriotic figures of eagles, flags, and Uncle Sam were produced along with American comic-strip characters. But by far the most treasured images were of Santa Claus, angels, songbirds and animals.

The art and techniques of making the molds for such glass ornaments have vanished over time, however some glassblowers still hold onto these cherished original molds. Today German glassblowers are once again making these creations for the American market in the same time-honored manner as their ancestors.

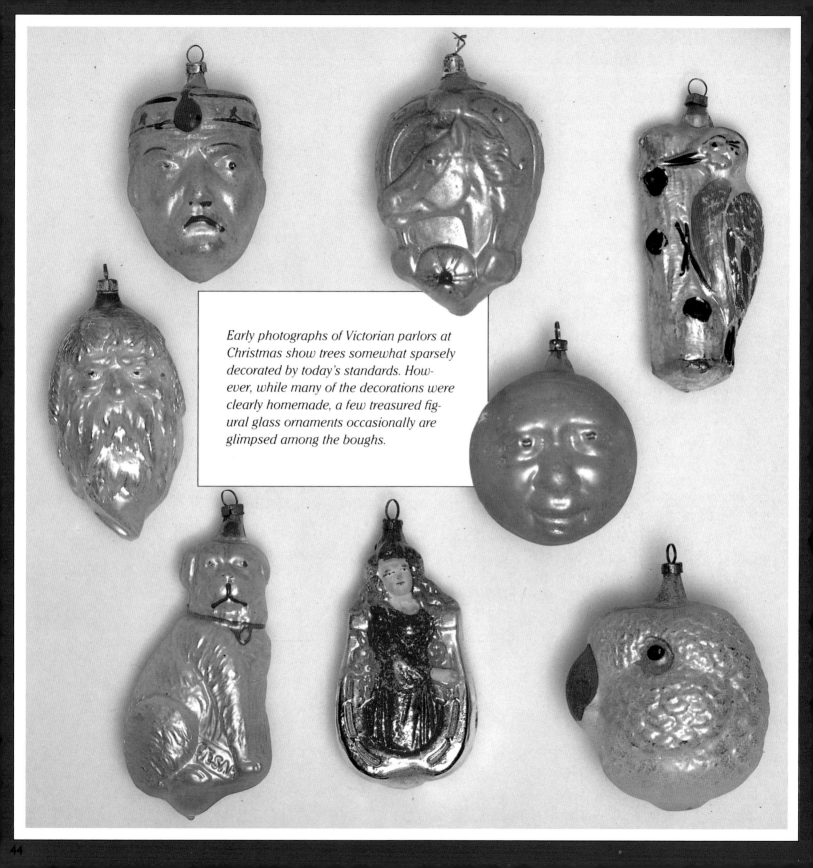

Early photographs of Victorian parlors at Christmas show trees somewhat sparsely decorated by today's standards. However, while many of the decorations were clearly homemade, a few treasured figural glass ornaments occasionally are glimpsed among the boughs.

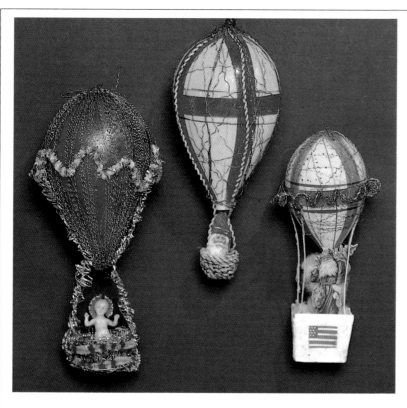

Popular public figures such as Al Jolson were immortalized in ornament form for the Christmas tree.

The world's fascination with flight around the turn of the century dates the airships shown above. Frequently, Santa Claus was included as a happy passenger. A tiny wax Baby Jesus takes flight in the hot air balloon at left.

Oddly, religious ornaments are relatively scarce. Joseph, the Christ Child, and the black Magi are depicted below.

Delicate glass shoes and a glass ribbon-wrapped blanket hold babies with lithographed die-cut paper faces (right).

Glass ornaments on metal clips add a festive look to the tree. Santa Claus and Little Red Riding Hood have applied glass eyes, and the gentleman dog sports a cardboard top hat. The angel has applied gold, embossed paper wings, and the turkey (far left) has a spun-glass tail.

A wooden ornament box from around 1900 gave its owner a convenient and safe way to store Christmas treasures from year to year.

These pear and apple ornaments have a metal clip at the top to hold a candle on the tree.

Blown glass ornaments depicting Uncle Sam were clearly made for the American market.

Far right: *An elaborate glass horn such as this could only be made by the most accomplished glassblowers. The boy is smiling on one side and crying on the other. When blown through, a tiny metal reed in the end of the horn actually whistles!*

The paper animals on the glass carousel exemplify the endless imagination and creativity of German artisans.

Before electric Christmas-tree lighting became available, candles were used to add illumination and beauty to the boughs. Figural glass candleholders were designed to hold a small taper in a metal clip at the base of the ornament. When lit, the candle's glow would light up the glass face of the figure. Some were hung from a branch by a fine wire and held oil and a small wick.

The angel that graced the top of the tree was often regarded as the most important decoration of all, a family's most treasured ornament. After the tree was lavishly decorated with ornaments and mementos carefully saved from year to year, the "tree-topper" was carefully placed at the apex of the tree where it would watch over the ensuing holiday festivities.

Made of wax, cotton, "Dresden" cardboard, or a combination of materials, each angel possessed its own expression and special Christmas charm.

A small tabletop Christmas tree fit securely into this German cast-iron tree stand. The basket on Santa's back held water to keep the tree fresh.

Among the most scarce and lovely antique Christmas decorations are embossed paper or cardboard ornaments known as "Dresdens." Manufactured primarily in Dresden and Leipzig, Germany, these decorations were made from the 1860s until the first World War.

Dresden ornaments were cleverly crafted and involved numerous time-consuming steps to reach completion. Finely detailed positive and negative molds were set into a large press. Thin cardboard sheets, moistened to make them pliable, were quickly stamped into the mold by a heavy press. When dry, the embossed pieces were given to cottage workers who did the finishing touches in their own homes.

The edges of the separate cardboard halves were trimmed, and the matching pieces were glued together to form a realistic figure. Each ornament rarely measured over four inches long. The majority of forms were either gilded or silvered to give them a shimmering surface. Other forms were elaborately painted by hand with realistic colors and shading.

No detail was too minute for the German artisans. A buffalo had a molting hide, a horse's head showed realistic veins in the neck, and a male human figure often sported a tiny moustache!

Frequently, a small pull-out cylinder or delicate colored-silk bag was inserted into the base or top of a decoration so that a sweet or small gift could be inserted. A miniature barometer might hold a candy box where the inner mechanism would be housed in a real one, or a one-inch-wide silk bag with drawstrings would be hidden in the neck of a reindeer's head.

Early store catalogs from the 1860s and '70s picture fanciful figural cardboard candy boxes and festive Christmas tree decorations. A page in an 1880s Ehrich's catalog shows a tree loaded with ornate cardboard ornaments and boxes and tiny gelatin flags. They were priced all the way from one cent to sixty cents for deluxe figures—clearly unaffordable for the average family.

During this same time period, elaborate ornaments of a different sort were being made in Sebnitz, Germany. Often called "Sebnitz" ornaments from their town of origin, these decorations were constructed of a fine wire frame filled with cotton batting around which thin, crinkly tinsel wire was tightly wrapped. Realistic miniature baby buggies and cribs holding one-inch wax babies also had cotton blankets and glass-bead handles or bedposts. Embossed silver-paper wheels ornamented cars and wagons. More scarce than Dresden ornaments, these fragile works of art truly capture the aura of a Victorian Christmas.

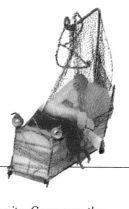

Made in the town of Sebnitz, Germany, the ornaments shown on this page are tiny works of art. Each measures no more than four inches in length, with some holding a one-inch wax baby or passenger. Sebnitz ornaments were handmade by cottage industry workers, so identical pieces are rarely found.

Miniature trains, boats, carriages, and buggies graced the Christmas trees of well-to-do American families in the 1880s and '90s. Each of those shown here is made of finely embossed paper or cardboard, including the tiny riders and horses. Some contain a hidden compartment for candy or a special gift. The largest ornament shown measures only five inches long.

Flat Dresden ornaments were manufactured during the same time period as three-dimensional ornaments. While they were attractive decorations for the Christmas tree, they also served as fine additions to a Victorian family's scrap album.

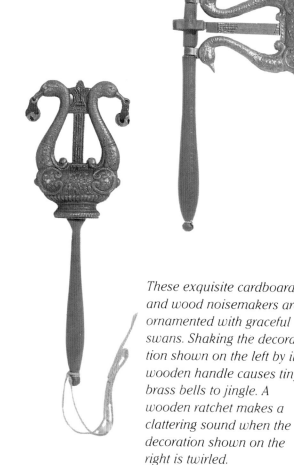

These exquisite cardboard and wood noisemakers are ornamented with graceful swans. Shaking the decoration shown on the left by its wooden handle causes tiny brass bells to jingle. A wooden ratchet makes a clattering sound when the decoration shown on the right is twirled.

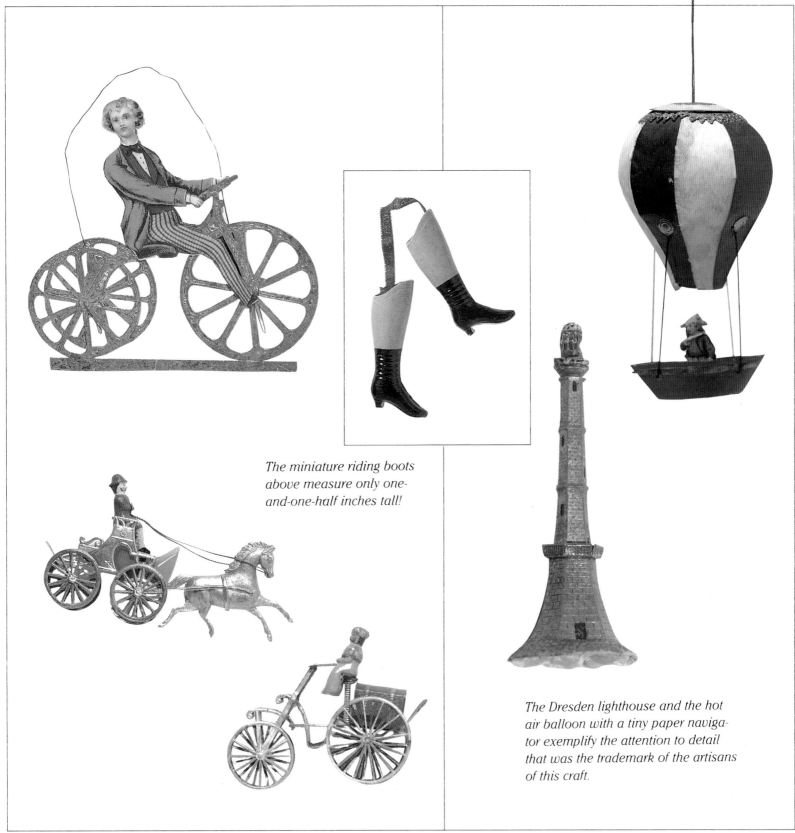

The miniature riding boots above measure only one-and-one-half inches tall!

The Dresden lighthouse and the hot air balloon with a tiny paper navigator exemplify the attention to detail that was the trademark of the artisans of this craft.

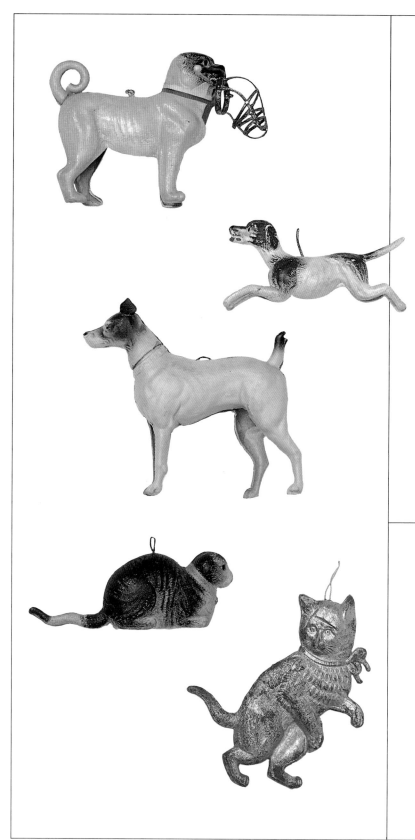

Embossed cardboard dogs and cats were hung from the green boughs of Victorian trees. Equestrians leaping tiny fences reflect the remarkable detail craftsmen applied to each ornament. The lady rider even wears a black velvet skirt!

Parrots, roosters and even a seahorse also adorned the trees of yesteryear.

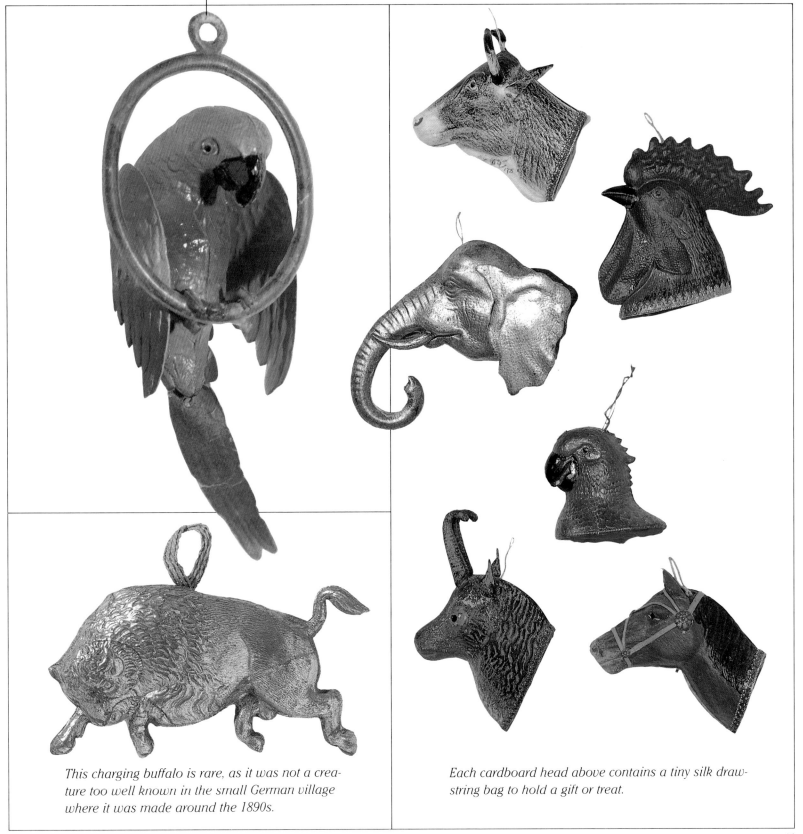

This charging buffalo is rare, as it was not a creature too well known in the small German village where it was made around the 1890s.

Each cardboard head above contains a tiny silk drawstring bag to hold a gift or treat.

At the turn of the century, when the German Christmas-decoration and toy industry was booming, cotton ornaments were among the more popular decorations exported to America. Made from puffy white cotton batting, they added a snowy, festive touch to the tree.

The making of cotton ornaments was a cottage industry in which families painstakingly assembled the figures by hand in their homes. Strips of cotton batting were wrapped tightly around and glued to a fine wire or cardboard frame in the shape of a human or animal. Facial features were handpainted, or a lithographed paper or composition "mask" face was applied with a drop of glue. The figures were then dressed in tiny crepe-paper clothes and trims. An elephant might be given a fancy paper blanket on its back or a lady an elaborate tasseled crepe-paper parasol. An angel, Santa Claus, or child in snow gear would often receive a thin coat of glue and a sprinkling of fine, sparkly mica flakes to give it a wintery appearance.

Fruits and vegetables made of cotton were among the most common yet lovely of the decorations available. Pears, apples, and sugarplums were sprayed with a blush of pink, yellow, blue, or green, and occasionally they were trimmed with a green-fabric leaf. Though simple, they were quite realistic.

A Christmas tree adorned with treasured ornaments was all the more beautiful ladened with these snow-white cotton figures.

Jolly cotton clowns and jesters made whimsical tree ornaments and served as unbreakable toys for the children. With heads made of papier-mâché, they were brightly painted, and a tiny wand, playing cards, or even a small metal tricycle could be added.

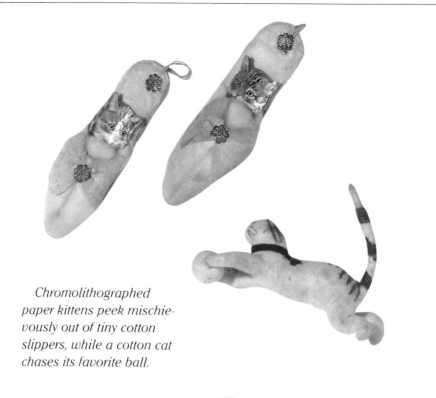

Chromolithographed paper kittens peek mischievously out of tiny cotton slippers, while a cotton cat chases its favorite ball.

Tradesmen at the turn of the century were depicted holding the fruits of their labor. Here a baker and a glassblower show off their wares.

Uncle Sam, at right, sports crepe-paper clothes, a paper top hat, and a tiny American flag.

Germans were fascinated by black Americans, as they represented a culture with which they were unfamiliar. Cotton black figures are scarce and were made primarily for the American market. Though the more stereotypical features on some of the figures are disturbing to modern sensibilities, they represent part of American history and views of the time.

The brown cotton rabbit carries a pack of tiny cotton carrots on his back.

Above: *German craftsmen created images in cotton that were familiar to children. Little Red Riding Hood and the wolf, a hen and her chicks, and Santa with toadstools (the latter a symbol of good luck in Germany) are each perched on a cardboard platform neatly wrapped in cotton.*

Mr. and Mrs. Rabbit go out for a Christmas stroll.

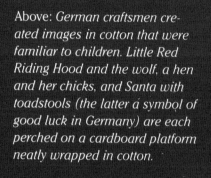

A cowboy with lasso on horseback.

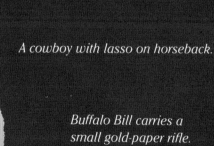

Buffalo Bill carries a small gold-paper rifle.

A ram wears a miniature gold bell on his collar.

Under the wintery coats of these cotton snowmen is a cardboard box for candies!

Children sometimes glued together carefully cut-out scraps of cotton batting and die-cut lithographed paper Santas and angels to make frosty tree decorations.

A cotton Santa, below, is well-equipped for winter fun with his blown-glass skiis and poles!

It was highly fashionable in well-to-do Victorian homes to adorn a dinner table with a small party favor for each guest. Women's publications of the day provided ideas and instructions on how to make by hand fancy boxes and containers for this purpose, and advertisers offered a mind-boggling assortment of candy boxes and bon-bonnieres one could purchase at the local mercantile or confectioner's shop.

A Victorian lady could buy fancy holly- or poinsettia-printed paper, lithographed paper "scraps," and tinsel trims to assemble cornucopias for use on the Christmas tree or as table favors. To the delight of children, Santa would often fill the cones that hung on the tree with peppermint sticks, hard candies, and nuts during his visit on Christmas Eve.

The finest of commercially

made candy containers at the turn of the century originated in Germany. Usually measuring only two or three inches across, these little boxes were made of cardboard or papier-mâché. The recipients could open the drawstring of a small silk bag or pull out a tiny sliding cylinder in the container to reveal a small gift or sweet placed there by the hostess.

Larger candy containers were made as table centerpieces or gifts for a very fortunate child. Designed to be refilled again and again, they could be used each holiday season. Such containers came in countless forms, including angels, children dressed in snowy outfits, and reindeer with removable heads.

Cottage artisans also created realistic miniature violins and banjos that pulled apart with fine paper frets and strings, two-inch suitcases with paper labels reflecting world destinations, small trolleys with windows, steps, and railings and a removable roof to reveal sweets inside, and even tiny shoes and slippers, each with a closable silk bag in the top.

Cardboard candy boxes with colorful lithographed Christmas images were occasionally given to children by schools and churches during the holidays. Many were designed to be hung on the tree by small string handles. Some, like that shown in the lower right corner on the previous page, combined religion with Christmas whimsy by depicting Santa emerging from the chimney of a church.

Right: *Papier-mâché children in snowy suits conceal small boxes for sweets, and two cotton children with bisque heads deliver sweets in their frosty log cart.*

A school of papier-mâché fish, each with a side flap that opens to hold candy.

Imagine the initial disappointment felt by the child who found this papier-mâché lump of coal in his stocking Christmas morning of 1878! At first believing that Santa Claus was indeed aware he had misbehaved during the year, he would be surprised to find a slide-out panel that revealed a small hoard of sweets!

Homemade colorful paper and tinsel cones hung from the tree and held nuts and hard candy.

Right: *A twenty-six-inch-tall jolly cotton snowman decorated in his Christmas finery hides a cylinder under his coat for several pounds of candy.*

Before electric lighting, lithographed tin clips were used to hold small white candles to the ends of branches of Christmas trees displayed in homes and churches alike.

Even when not serving their primary function of holding a lighted candle upright on the tree, the more elaborate of candleholders made beautiful decorations. Most were fashioned of lithographed tin and were two-sided, so they were attractive no matter where they were placed on the tree. Some, like the heart and Santa Claus shown here, were made of a composition of paper pulp and glue and painted gold.

Despite their remarkable detail, figural Christmas lights originally sold for only a few cents. Although the bulbs were relatively inexpensive, a family still had to be well-to-do in the early 1900s to afford enough of them to make an effective display.

On the Christmas tree, Uncle Sam and Miss Liberty glowed side-by-side with Mary and Joseph (below), comical and whimsical characters, and even a witch.

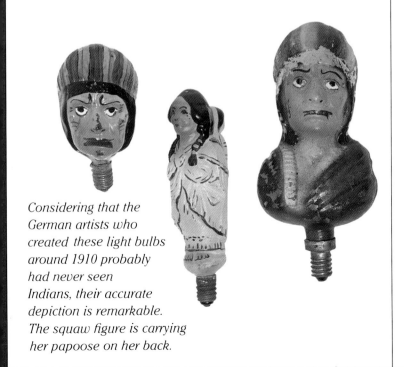

Considering that the German artists who created these light bulbs around 1910 probably had never seen Indians, their accurate depiction is remarkable. The squaw figure is carrying her papoose on her back.

In the nineteenth century, German Christmas trees were ornamented with homemade cookies, paper and ribbon decorations, fruit and nuts, and small white candles—which when lit held appreciative celebrants in awe. Since trees at that time were freshly cut on Christmas Eve and immediately decorated, accidents from fire were few. Candles are still used on the tree occasionally in Germany for special celebrations, although strings of realistic-looking electric candles are far more popular.

Candles were fastened to a tree's branches by a wide variety of cleverly designed clips and holders, often counterbalanced by a heavy clay or pot metal form that hung on a wire below the candleholder. This weight, shaped like a ball or star or pinecone, kept the candle balanced and upright on a branch, thereby reducing the risk of fire. Some candleholders had counterbalances made of lithographed tin embossed with the shapes of angels, hearts or Santa Clauses.

Many candle-clips were tin and commercially produced, the simplest of them embossed and "washed" in silver or gold paints. More elaborate candle-clips were made of colorful lithographed tin.

An electrically illuminated Christmas tree was first displayed in New York City in 1882. In subsequent years, festoons of electric lights became available to the public and were eagerly acquired. Around 1904, Christmas tree lights in figural shapes were first manufactured in Austria, and German glassblowers were quick to seize upon this clever innovation. Made of clear glass, the figures were delicately painted and glowed softly among the tree branches. Punch and Judy, clowns, animals of all kinds, and countless other figures appeared as light bulbs.

By 1920, Japanese manufacturers had recognized the huge potential market in America for figural Christmas lights and had begun copying many of the most popular German designs. Unlike the European prototypes, which were made of painted clear glass with the screw-in base at bottom, the Japanese lights primarily were made of milk glass and screwed into the sockets at the top. This simple change made Japanese lights easier to use since they did not have to be balanced upright on a branch.

The Japanese developed many of their own designs and produced figural lights in greatest quantity during the 1920s and '30s, with some even available into the 1950s. However, when a single bulb burned out, its entire string of lights ceased to work. The bad bulb had to be replaced by a good one before the string lit up again. Because these bulbs burned rather hot and were a potential fire hazard, they faded from popularity to be replaced by the simply shaped and single colored bulbs of today.

Few decorations contribute more to the beauty, excitement, and wonder of Christmas than twinkling lights on an evergreen tree. While the use of candles is not viewed as safe today, and figural lights are no longer commonplace, the rare tree decorated in this old-fashioned way generates gasps of appreciation from those fortunate enough to view it.

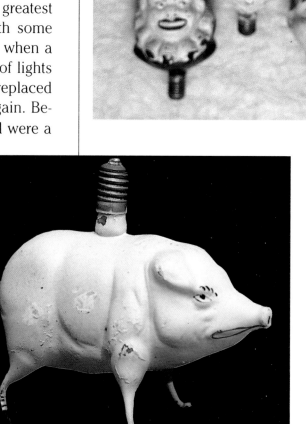

Above: *Comical faces, jolly clowns, and angelic children smile continuously to cheer Christmas celebrants.*

This realistic but rather fierce-looking pig was made in Germany around 1910. It is extremely unusual in that it has extended glass legs.

The imagination of glassblowers seems to have been endless. At left, an elderly gentleman in spectacles plays his bass fiddle while a Brownie and a pig show off their holiday outfits.

Lights designed as nursery rhyme characters such as Little Miss Muffet and Puss 'n Boots (lower left) were quickly identified by observant boys and girls.

Below: European figural lights were made in much the same way as the glass ornaments. A heated clear-glass tube was mouth-blown into a claylike mold. When cooled, the bulb was painted by hand. The filament and screw-in base were then attached with a gluelike plaster.

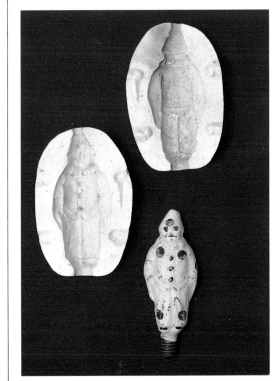

Figural Christmas light bulbs made of milk glass were developed by the Japanese in the 1920s for export to America. Literally hundreds of different figures were produced. Because they were inexpensive, they were often discarded when they burned out.

Standing two feet tall, this German glass Santa Claus was a store-window display in the early 1900s. Two cylindrical light bulbs inside illuminate his face and body.

In contrast to the fine European Christmas lights shown on the opposite page, Japanese bulbs tended to be less detailed. However, their whimsical appeal made them tremendously popular.

Lower left: *Made by Noma in Japan for the Canadian market, this set included a totem pole, an Eskimo, Indians, a Mountie, and a beaver grasping a branch.*

Many characters popular with children were depicted in the form of figural Christmas-tree lights. At left are Mickey Mouse, Pinocchio, Goofy, Dopey, Donald Duck holding a candy cane, Minnie Mouse with a Christmas present, Pluto, and Jiminy Cricket.

Snow White and the Seven Dwarfs have long been storybook favorites. These Christmas light bulbs, depicting each of the different characters, were sold as sets.

Although they are quite appealing, like other old figural light bulbs they tended to burn very hot, and when any one bulb burned out, the remainder of the string would not light.

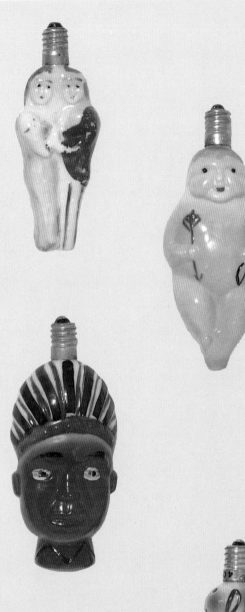

Figural light bulbs by the Stanley Company (above) were made with much attention to detail.

Some of the Christmas light images created by the Japanese are now difficult to identify. However, familiar characters such as members of the Howdy Doody gang (right) are still easily recognized.

SANTA CLAUS PUZZLE BOX

HOME

SANTA CLAUS SCROLL PUZZLE

M'LOUGHLIN BROS. New York

. . .and

to all a

good night!

CHRISTMAS PIE

CHINESE & SANTA CLAUS PUZZLE

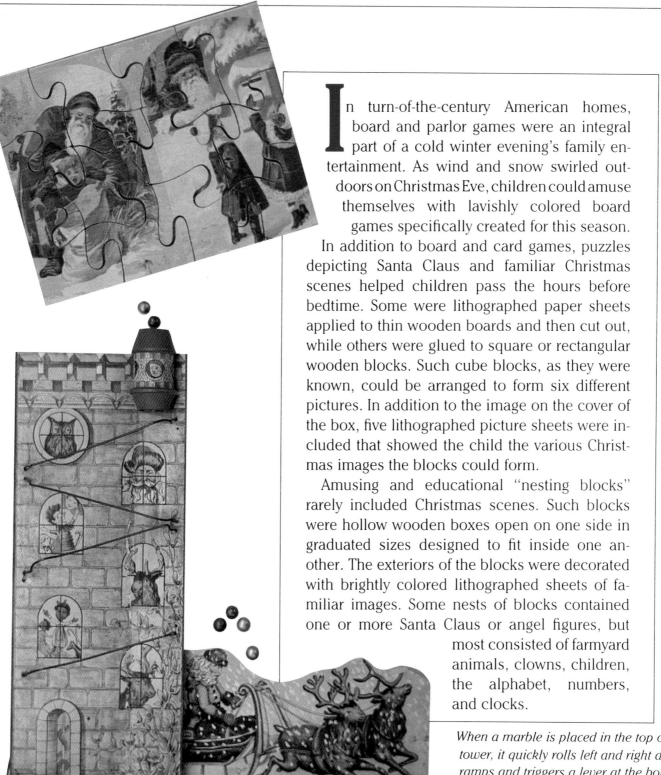

In turn-of-the-century American homes, board and parlor games were an integral part of a cold winter evening's family entertainment. As wind and snow swirled outdoors on Christmas Eve, children could amuse themselves with lavishly colored board games specifically created for this season.

In addition to board and card games, puzzles depicting Santa Claus and familiar Christmas scenes helped children pass the hours before bedtime. Some were lithographed paper sheets applied to thin wooden boards and then cut out, while others were glued to square or rectangular wooden blocks. Such cube blocks, as they were known, could be arranged to form six different pictures. In addition to the image on the cover of the box, five lithographed picture sheets were included that showed the child the various Christmas images the blocks could form.

Amusing and educational "nesting blocks" rarely included Christmas scenes. Such blocks were hollow wooden boxes open on one side in graduated sizes designed to fit inside one another. The exteriors of the blocks were decorated with brightly colored lithographed sheets of familiar images. Some nests of blocks contained one or more Santa Claus or angel figures, but most consisted of farmyard animals, clowns, children, the alphabet, numbers, and clocks.

When a marble is placed in the top of the tower, it quickly rolls left and right down the wire ramps and triggers a lever at the bottom. Suddenly, Santa Claus and his reindeer drop to the right from behind the tower!

With the exception of the mother decorating the tree, each of the family members in the mechanical picture at right move when the clock-work mechanism is wound. Santa Claus disappears and then gradually reappears in the window. Constructed of lithographed paper on wood, this American-made piece from the 1880s came self-framed and provided a family with hours of amusement.

Right: *A simple paper-covered wooden box presents a Christmas surprise when out pops Santa and a tiny reindeer. The inside of the box lid is decorated with "snow" to give Santa a wintery background.*

The Schoenhut Co. of Philadelphia produced this papier-mâché roly-poly Santa Claus at the turn of the century.

Santa Claus jumps out of a box in this early version of a Christmas Jack-in-the-box.

American manufacturer J. H. Singer produced the picture puzzle above in 1891. McLoughlin Bros. of New York, a maker of quality Christmas puzzles and blocks, produced the St. Nicholas puzzle below.

Most Santa block sets contained pictures of Santa Claus carrying out his Christmas duties.

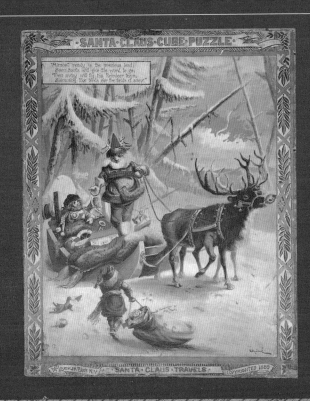

Puzzle blocks came in a wooden box that contained several cubes of wood covered with lithographed sheets that could form six different scenes.

By the light of kerosene lamps, Victorian children played board games to wile away the hours before the arrival of St. Nicholas. Although the games were played by simple rules that would not retain a modern child's interest for long, the vibrant lithographed color images continue to be captivating. The object of "The Visit of Santa Claus" at left is to get the jolly old fellow to bring presents to your house while bypassing your neighbors' homes!

Prominent American manufacturers of the era included McLoughlin Brothers, Parker Brothers, and Milton Bradley. Each made several different board and card games with a Christmas motif.

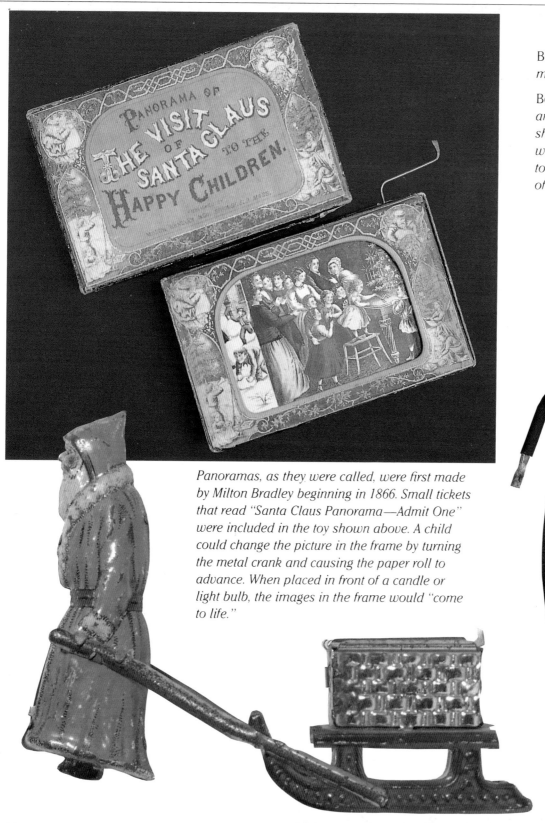

Below left: *A Santa marionette puppet made in America about 1885.*

Below right: *A photographer could amuse a child sitting for his portrait by shaking this Santa forward and backward, causing a small bellows inside to squeak, or by blowing into the end of the wooden whistle.*

Panoramas, as they were called, were first made by Milton Bradley beginning in 1866. Small tickets that read "Santa Claus Panorama—Admit One" were included in the toy shown above. A child could change the picture in the frame by turning the metal crank and causing the paper roll to advance. When placed in front of a candle or light bulb, the images in the frame would "come to life."

Left: *Known as a "penny toy" because it could be purchased for one cent, this three-inch-tall tin Santa held candy under the slide-out top of his sled.*

A store merchant in the late nineteenth century would have been sure to attract customers with this mechanical display in his window. When the clockwork mechanism is wound, the lithographed paper-on-wood figures move to and fro. Gradually, Santa Claus lifts the jester out of his bag to the children's delight. After the clown's arms and legs are extended, Santa suddenly drops him back into his bag for the action to begin anew!

My heartfelt thanks go to Jos. Trautwein for having encouraged me to do this book. Without his enthusiasm, creative talent, tireless efforts, and, most important, his love of Christmas, this book would not have been possible. For his invaluable editorial assistance, advice, and creative input, I thank Walton Rawls of Abbeville Press. Very special thanks to Cor Videler for his considerable photography skills and consistently happy and patient disposition. And thanks to the staff of Abbeville Press for all of their hard work.

I am very grateful to other authors who researched the heritage of antique Christmas decorations, and shared their collections and findings with others, and particularly to Philip V. Snyder, Eva Stille, and John Grossman. My thanks also to Rich Giger for his unending support, Rita Trautwein for her patience and understanding, and Jim Morrison for his constant encouragement and knowledge.

And, finally, my deepest thanks to all of the Christmas collector friends and antique Christmas decorations dealers who have assisted me in my collecting efforts over the years, as well as to the many families who unwittingly preserved a part of history by saving and cherishing their family Christmas decorations so they can be enjoyed by future generations.

Small ceramic flasks, sometimes called "nips," were given to customers by innkeepers and pub owners around 1900. This Santa Claus flask held a few sips of Christmas cheer.

The photographic illustrations were supervised by Jos. Trautwein and recorded on film by Cor Videler. All items shown are from the antique Christmas collection of Robert M. Merck.